The

WORST-CASE SCENARIO
Survival Handbook:

GROSS

Junior Edition

The
WORST-CASE SCENARIO
Survival Handbook:

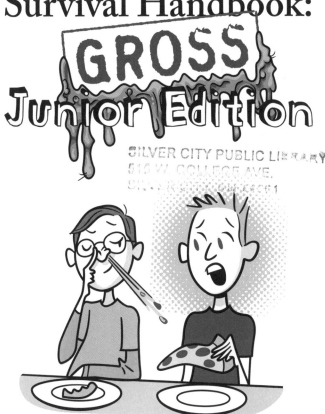

GROSS

Junior Edition

By David Borgenicht, Nathaniel Marunas, and Robin Epstein

Illustrated by Chuck Gonzales

chronicle books · san francisco

A WORD OF WARNING: It's always important to keep safety in mind. If you're careless, even the tamest activities can result in injury. As such, all readers are urged to act with caution, ask for adult advice, obey all laws, and respect the rights of others when handling any Worst-Case Scenario.

Library of Congress Cataloging-in-Publication Data available.
ISBN: 978-0-8118-7570-7

Book design by Lynne Yeamans.
Typeset in Adobe Garamond, Blockhead, and Imperfect.
Illustrations by Chuck Gonzales.

Manufactured by Toppan Leefung, Da Ling Shan Town, Dongguan, China, in June 2010.

10 9 8 7 6 5 4 3 2 1

This product conforms to CPSIA 2008.

Chronicle Books LLC
680 Second Street, San Francisco, California 94107

www.chroniclekids.com

CONTENTS

CHAPTER 4

Gross Is All Around You

What is that smell?

You sniff the air, suddenly aware that something evil must have farted right near you. You get another whiff and—oh no...no...NO! That smell is coming from the bottom of your shoe! You look up to shake your fist at the sky for putting the mother lode of dog poop in your path when—*splat!*—a stream of hot, oozing bird poop hits you in the eye. Sick! A pre-barf burp starts rising in your throat. You can feel you're about to lose your lunch—but ack!—there's no toilet or trash can in sight. What are you going to do?!

Well that's where this book comes in handy! This guide has all the tips for how to survive the grossest of the gross situations that life poops out at you.

But be warned: This book is beyond sick. It's *disgusting*. And chances are, not only will you gag at its grossness, you will also want to put down that snack while reading it. Unless, of course, you think you can handle eating while learning about floods of blood, pus-filled wounds, hairy food, and roach invasions.

Scores of other revolting facts are also packed into these pages. Have you ever wondered how many insect legs the government officially allows in peanut butter? Or why the dung beetle loves poop so much? You'll soon find out.

You can turn to this book for tips on how to survive when, say, a tick buries its head in your leg to feast on your blood. Or when your friend has such terrible breath, you can't even

remember your own name, let alone what you were just talking about. Or when you accidentally touch that germy gum under your desk at school, or want to find a stall in the school bathroom that isn't totally disgusting.

But say a spray of mucus comes shooting out of *your* nose. Or a huge gassy burp bubbles up in the middle of *your* piano recital. How will *you* handle zombie breath when it happens to you? This book will not only tell you how to deal, it'll give tips on how to curb the mind-melting embarrassment that can arise from this stuff, too.

With an incredible blend of disgusting facts, stomach-turning medical conditions, and details on revolting animal behavior, this guide's got it all. It's the ultimate survival guide when life coughs up something so nasty that even the dog won't eat it.

—*David Borgenicht, Nathaniel Marunas, and Robin Epstein*

CHAPTER 1

The Human Body

How to Cope with Nightmare Boogers

You—yes, you—have nature's very own flypaper stuck up your nose! We're *snot* kidding. Snot, aka mucus, aka a nose loogie, can be watery clear or goopy green, and—surprise—it's actually good for something! It catches dirt, germs, and the other cruddy stuff in the air you breathe, then tries to shoot it out your body in one totally gross strand of slime. When it dries out, hello boogers! Here's how to deal with snot of all sorts.

1 Vent one nostril at a time.

If you've got boulder-sized boogers jammed up your nose-hole, grab a tissue and get ready to roar, "Thar she blows!" First, push your clear nostril shut with one thumb. With your other hand, cover the stuffed nostril with the tissue. And then, on the count of three, give a powerful snort through the blocked hole. By blasting air through one vent instead of two, you give more velocity (power) to that snot rocket.

2 Build an excavator.

If that stubborn boogie still won't budge, make yourself a booger scooper. (Note: Do *not* confuse this with your dog's pooper scooper.) Fold a tissue in half, grab the center of the fold, then twist the folded halves into a long poker. Dab the tip with a drop of water and—*voilà*—you've got a single-use boogie pick stick.

Nostril Venting

Push your clear nostril shut.

Blow a powerful snort through the blocked nostril.

③ The brain drain.

Crusty boogers are one thing, but sometimes it seems like the contents of your head are sliding out your nose. Turn the tide on this river of goop by adding (yes) *more* moisture to the mix. Steam—from hot showers, drinks, and soups—actually helps to thin your mucus and de-gunk your blowholes faster.

> **BE AWARE** • You can get a runny nose not just from *having* a cold but from *being* cold. Normally, tiny hairlike structures (cilia) brush the snot and germs down your throat. But when cilia get sluggish in low temperatures, snot starts streaming out your nostrils.

What to Say When You Get Busted Digging for Gold

If someone spots you poking around in your snot pot, you can always save the situation with a snappy response. Try one of these.

- "The back of my eyeball was itchy."
- "I lost a contact lens."
- "I tripped and fell on my finger."
- "My brain was loose—I had to tuck it back into place."
- "My finger was cold."

A Field Guide to Boogers and Snot

	• The Brown Nugget. The most common booger, a pebble of dried-up snot and dirt.
	• The Corn Flake. A flat, golden sheet of dried-up snot. This is one nugget you don't want in your cereal.
	• The Bat in the Cave. A Corn Flake or Brown Nugget stuck to one of the tiny hairs in your nose; generally removed by hand.
	**• The Slimy Earthworm.** A ropy strand of snot that resembles a magician's never-ending handkerchief trick when pulled out of your nose.
	• The Yellow River. Yellowish, runny mucus may be a sign your immune system is fighting a cold or sinus infection.
	• The Green Gobbets. Your snot turns into this gummy, gray-green mass toward the end of a cold, when the dead germs and excess mucus really pile up in your nostrils.

How to Survive a Barf Emergency

Something is *not* right in your stomach. Wait—maybe it's a little higher up.... *Ugh*, now sour-tasting saliva is pooling at the back of your throat.... *Uh-oh*, you're about to blow chunks! Here's how to keep your cool the next time you lose your lunch.

1 Know the signs.

It feels like your stomach's on a roller-coaster ride. Suddenly you're sweaty or maybe you get the chills, but the temperature hasn't changed. Your heart's pounding, and your head's aching. Well, get ready, because these are your body's early warning signs that a vomit volcano might soon erupt. Brace yourself.

2 Get to a vessel.

Barf waits for no man (or girl or boy). So if you're nowhere near a bathroom when the mighty chunks get set to spew, use these options as last-ditch hurl-atoriums:

Try a trash can; use the "kitchen sink" approach—everything winds up in there eventually; or find a plastic or paper bag, put it around your mouth, drop your head forward, and inflate like a balloon. As last resorts, puke into a plant pot, tote bag, or baseball cap. And, if you're really stuck, do the old heave-ho into a fishbowl.

Barf Vessels (in Decreasing Order of Brilliance)

Trash can   Paper bag   Umbrella stand   Your brother's backpack

Strike a (puking) pose.

Occasionally you get little or no prep time before the spew starts to surge. Here's how to minimize the mess to your pride *and* your shoes.

1. **Crouch.** Staying low to the ground makes for a smaller splash when the molten mush crashes to Earth.

2. **Bend at the waist.** This will prevent upchucking (i.e., puking) out your nose, which almost makes barfing through your mouth a picnic!

Barfonyms

Vomit comes in many shapes, sizes, and flavors. It's only fitting that there should be an equal number of ways to describe the 3-D burp.

- Blow chunks
- Bow down before the porcelain god
- Dinner revisited
- Emesis (the medical term for throwing up)
- Gack
- Gargle gravy
- Heave
- Hurl
- Keck
- Lose your lunch
- Ralph
- Regurgitate
- Retch
- Spew
- Technicolor yawn
- Toss your cookies
- Whistle beef
- Yak

Vomit on Board

Ocean motion, highway havoc, air activity—all these things can make your belly back-flip. Here's how to avoid the Big Heave-Ho.

- **Eye the horizon.** Taking your focus off the passing landscape (like if you're reading) can send your brain mixed signals and make you motion sick: Your eyes think you're in a fixed place because the book isn't moving. But your inner ear senses the car traveling. That combo is a recipe for retching.

- **Face front.** Face the direction you're going to realign your eye and ear motion sensors.

- **Eat up.** A light snack helps, especially if you haven't eaten for several hours. Bland food, like toast or crackers, and room-temperature water or ginger ale will alleviate hunger pangs, which can make you feel even worse than you already do.

How to Survive Bad Breath

Your friend's breath is so bad that when he speaks, it smells like his face farted. His breath is so stinky, you don't know whether to offer him gum or toilet paper. And lucky you! He is in an extremely chatty mood—today, and every day. Here's how to make it through a conversation without coughing up your breakfast, lunch, and last night's dinner.

Surviving Your Friend's Breath

STEP 1
Breathe through your mouth.

STEP 2
Offer a stick of minty-fresh gum.

① Breathe through your mouth.

Sometimes your best bet is the most simple: avoid using your nose by breathing through your mouth. The less you sniff, the better you'll be, but if that isn't enough...

② Offer a refresh "mint."

If you happen to have a pack of gum or some mints, break them out, pop one in your mouth, then tell your friend that it's *the best tasting mint ever*! Then say, "Here, you gotta see for yourself!" But if you're mint-less...

③ Offer a refreshment.

Maybe you don't have any gum or mints, or your friend is anti-candy. In that case, offer him a beverage. Swallowing washes away stanky mouth bacteria. Say, "Whew, I'm thirstier than a fish in a desert. I'm gonna get a glass of water, and I'll grab one for you, too."

> **BE AWARE** • Another common source of bad breath is the nose. Sinus infections and misplaced foreign objects can cause a stench that would make a vulture pass out.

Stand back.

Sadly, someone with a toe-curling case of Stench Mouth can fill an entire room with the evil fog. But sometimes, just a few steps is all it takes. So make like a vampire slayer with a fistful of garlic and keep backing away until you've made your escape from Count Stinkula.

Good Morning, Stinkyhead!

The reason morning breath is so incredibly gross is simple: During the day, we produce (and swallow) large amounts of saliva, which washes bacteria and food away from our mouths and down to our stomachs. When we're asleep, our bodies stop making and swallowing all that saliva, which leaves the stinking bacteria to roam free all night long!

How to Deal When You Have Bad Breath

Gross as it is when the smell of half-digested roadkill wafts your way, remember that bad breath happens to good people—tomorrow, it might be *you* with the kind of breath that could level a city block. Here's how to deal when *you're* the one who gets offered a mint...or two...or three...

1 See if you stink.

The surest way to tell if you've got death breath is to ask someone to take a whiff. AWKWARD! So here's how to check your PSF (Personal Stink Factor) for yourself.

1. With a clean fingertip, collect some saliva from the back of your tongue (don't make yourself throw up!), and rub it on the back of your other hand.

2. Wait for the patch of spit to dry, then give it a whiff. If it smells like wet dog, it's time to take action.

② Keep your mouth clean.

Halitosis is caused by the millions of bacteria partying day and night on your tongue, gums, and teeth. So if your breath reeks, it's usually because of less-than perfect gum and tooth maintenance (Exhibit A: your dog's breath—how often does *he* brush?). If you were looking for a good reason to keep a travel toothbrush and dental floss in your backpack, this is it. (Brush the back of your tongue, too—it's the food court at the local mall, as far as bacteria are concerned.)

Clean-Mouth Arsenal

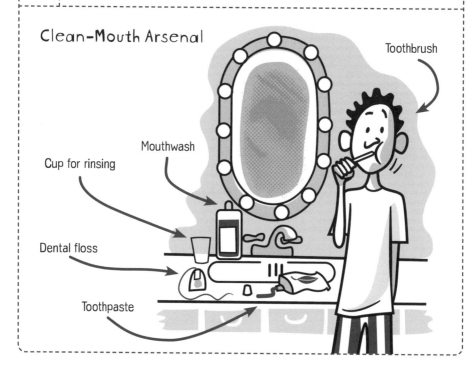

Toothbrush

Mouthwash

Cup for rinsing

Dental floss

Toothpaste

3 Cover it up.

If you can't get to a bathroom for some emergency mouth maintenance, you can, of course, pop a sugar-free breath strip or mint.

For some natural breath fresheners, try these options:

- **Fresh herbs.** Not just for garnishing plates, parsley is also a temporary remedy for bad breath (it masks the smell). Spearmint and rosemary will also work in a pinch.
- **Fruits and vegetables.** Eating apples, celery, and carrots helps your mouth produce saliva, which clears away the stinky bacteria.
- **Water.** Wash bad breath bacteria away by drinking water throughout the day. That's right—drown your bad breath!

FAST FACT • Four out of five bacteria prefer sugar to all other foods, so always opt for sugar-free mints and gum to keep the bacteria that cause bad breath from rocking out in your mouth.

Foods That Make You Stinky

You can brush from here to kingdom come, but if you chew on these foods before getting into a crowded car, you might be forced to ride on the roof. Here's a short list of foods to avoid.

- **Foods with onion or garlic.** Onions and garlic have stinky compounds that enter your bloodstream and are breathed out through your lungs.

- **Fishy foods, meats, eggy foods, and cheese.** Bacteria love the amino acids found in these protein-rich foods.

- **Citrus juices.** Citric acid makes your mouth bacteria-friendly.

How to Survive a Monster Sneeze

Your friend's got a cold but still wants to hang out. He's sniffling, snorting, and sneezing, and his nose is a germ factory. Even if you're the kind of friends who share everything, this is something better kept to himself. Here's how to stay out of the way of his spray.

1 Tell him to go for the elbow.

Though covering a sneeze with a hand stops the free blast of germs, everything touched later gets coated with nasal crud. So tell your friend to sneeze into his elbow, covering his nose and mouth Dracula-style instead.

2 Stay out of the zone.

The saliva, mucus, and germ combo released from one mighty sneeze can travel 5 feet (1.5 meters) from the sneezer's nose. If you're with a reckless sneezer, step back as far as you can when you sense the horn's about to blow, or you'll need to take action.

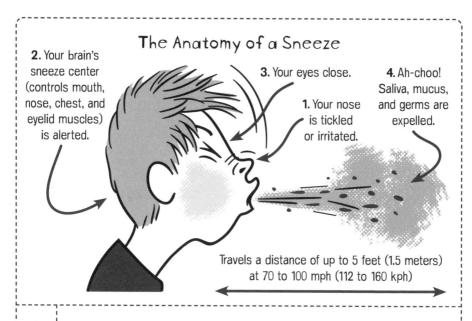

The Anatomy of a Sneeze

2. Your brain's sneeze center (controls mouth, nose, chest, and eyelid muscles) is alerted.

3. Your eyes close.

1. Your nose is tickled or irritated.

4. Ah-choo! Saliva, mucus, and germs are expelled.

Travels a distance of up to 5 feet (1.5 meters) at 70 to 100 mph (112 to 160 kph)

③ Wash those germs away.

Scrub any part of you that got sprayed (whether it feels wet or not). And don't be shy with the soap: rub it around for at least twenty seconds—long enough to sing the alphabet song. Slowly. And if you saw that a table or desk got sprayed, clean that off, too. Since germs can live on surfaces for hours, the next person who comes along would never know that Viruspalooza is taking place all around them.

FAST FACT • "Photic sneezers" are people who sneeze when they look at the sun or a bright light.

Gesundheit!
and Other Ways to Greet the Sneeze

In some countries, people don't say anything to a sneezer other than the universally accepted *"Eeeewww!"* But most cultures have a tradition of saying *something*—usually a blessing of health. Here is a sampling of who says what, where.

COUNTRY	BLESSING	HOW TO SAY IT	WHAT IT MEANS
Brazil	*Saúde!*	SOW-djeh	Health!
Sweden	*Prosit!*	PRO-set	Health!
France	*À vos souhaits!*	Ah vōz sway	May your wishes come true!
Germany	*Gesundheit!*	Geh-ZOONT-hīt	Health!
Italy	*Salute!*	Sah-LOO-teh	Health!
Poland	*Na zdrowie!*	Nah z-drōv-EE-eh	Health!
Spain	*¡Salud!*	Sah-LOOD	Health!

How to Deal with a Spit Talker

That's funny, did it suddenly start raining? *Indoors?* No, it's just your friend, coating your face with little flecks of spittle. You know, spit. It's that frothy, slimy mixture that's 98 percent water and 2 percent GROSS, including mucus, bacteria, enzymes that help the digestive process, and all the other junk you've been eating and breathing. Here are some strategies for surviving a conversation with a walking, talking lawn sprinkler.

1 Step back—*way* back.

The second the spit starts to fly, be sure to put at least an arm's length between you and the source. Unless he's *trying* to spit in your face, random showers shouldn't travel any farther than that. With any luck, this will send a signal to your friend that he should stop giving you the unofficial weather report.

2 Mime your way out of trouble.

You might be surprised by how effective a small swipe with an index finger to the face can be. Be chill about it; there's no need to embarrass the person. Just send

the signal that you got hit with friendly fire. Without words, this will indicate that you don't want to make a big deal about it, but you DO need it to stop.

3 Use an excuse.

If the nonverbal approach isn't working, you'll have to resort to words to get you back on dry land. Try telling the spitter that you don't want him to get too close because you might have a cold coming on, and you'd hate for him to catch it. No need to mention that such future illness will probably come from his spittle landing in your eye.

4 Tell the truth.

If you still find yourself being soaked in spit, telling the truth just might be the only way to stop the spray. Politely inform the person that while you like animals as much as the next person, you'd prefer *not* to have your faced washed like a lion cub being cleaned by its mama.

Gross Things Animals Do with Spit

- **Disinfect wounds.** Mice, dogs, and other animals lick their wounds to clean them—and some even have chemical compounds in their saliva that speed healing.

- **Build nests.** Some species of *Aerodramus* swiftlet (a small bird native to East Asia and Australia) build their nests entirely out of their thick spit, which hardens on contact with air. These nests are the main ingredient in the Chinese delicacy called Bird's Nest Soup.

- **Subdue prey.** Many snakes and lizards have venomous saliva, which they use to paralyze or kill their prey. The Rinkhals Spitting Cobra can hit a person in the eye from 10 feet (3 meters) away.

- **Startle and scold.** Rather than fight, camels eject a powerful stream of spit *mixed with vomit* to startle or drive away other animals. Including people.

How to Survive a Bloody Nose

There you are, reading about World War II when all of a sudden, a bright red splatter appears on the page. Then another. And another! Sure, history can be colorful, but in this case, you have a leaky blood vessel in your nose. Don't panic—here's how to dam the red river.

1 Sit tight and upright.

Blood vessels are like plumbing: just as it takes more effort to pump water to the top floor of a house, your heart won't pump as much blood out your nose if you keep your head above your heart. Also, lean forward so the blood drains out of your nose—*not* back in.

2 Pinch your nose.

Help the broken blood vessel in your nose to clot (that's when blood thickens) by slowing the blood flow to the area. To do this, pinch the soft parts of your nose together and up against the bony part for a solid five minutes (if you keep letting go, Old Faithful will keep gushing).

3 Freeze your cheeks.

Another way to slow the flow of vampire juice is to put ice wrapped in a plastic bag or thin towel on your nose and cheeks. This will shrink the blood vessels in your sinuses and help limit the blood flow.

4 Make a nose plug.

If the pinching and freezing don't do the trick, you may have to make a nasal dam. Crumple some soft, clean tissue paper into a fingertip-sized plug and gently

wedge it into your nostril. If you have a real gusher, you may need one for each blowhole. Note: You will look like a stuffed animal whose brains fell out of its nose. But, hey, at least your clothes won't have the blood-splattered look.

No Nosebleeds, Please!

Since there are so many blood vessels in our noses that are close to the surface of the skin, it's a miracle we don't get bloody noses all the time. Here's how to avoid them.

 • **Drink plenty of water.** When you're dehydrated, the skin in your nose becomes dry and bloody.

 • **Steam up your sinuses.** Use a humidifier at night to keep things moisturized—especially in cold weather and high altitudes.

 • **Don't pick your nose.** Your fingernails can cause cuts to the sensitive skin up there.

 • **Avoid getting punched in the sniffer.** 'Nuff said.

How to Deal with a Gas Leak

That three-bean cheese burrito might not have been the best idea…. But it's too late for that thought. Now, you have more gas flowing through your guts than the local gas station. Unfortunately, you can be assured that gas is plotting a noisy escape through your butt crack. So here's what to do when your body turns into a fart factory.

❶ Wait—then evacuate!

Once you've *cut the cheese* and let her rip, step away from the area you've skunked. But wait a second or two post-spray to make sure the gas has completely left your pants. Otherwise you risk carrying the stink with you to your new location.

> **FAST FACT** • When you smell a fart, you are breathing in gas particles, or "farticles," made by the bacteria in your butt.

❷ Say, "What?"

The first thing most people do when they fart (or flatulate) is to make a big show of being disgusted by the terrible odor. (This is where the phrase "He who smelt it, dealt it" comes from.) The pro strategy is to carry on like nothing happened and wait until someone else acts all grossed out before saying, "Hey, yeah! *Gross!* Who would *do* such a thing?!"

❸ Blame the nearest pet.

A dog is known as man's best friend for a reason. After you rip a smelly one, wait a few seconds, then grab your nose, point at the family pooch, and say, "Oh, man, *Knuckles*—that's *disgusting*!" The dog won't care as long as you give him an extra belly rub later for taking the blame. Note: Hard to pull off if the pet is a guinea pig or smaller.

4 Forgo farty foods.

The "my doggie did it" excuse will only work so many times. For future "toot" management, you might need to cut out certain foods known for their high fart content.

- **Cruciferous vegetables.** They may be good for you, but eating cauliflower, broccoli, cabbage, and turnips won't be good for those around you.

- **Meats.** This is why carnivores, like cats and dogs, have such stinky farts.

- **Eggs.** They already smell like farts when they're hard-boiled. *Not* a good sign.
- **Dairy products.** Sure, they help build bones, but they also make you break wind.
- **Beans.** Beans, beans, they're "the musical fruit… the more you eat, the more you toot." Though they don't make for really smelly farts, they're famous toot makers because they contain sugars our bodies can't easily digest.

The World's Greatest Fartiste

Joseph Pujol (1857–1945) was a Frenchman who had a world-spanning career as a flatulist (someone who farts on stage professionally). He came to fame at the legendary Moulin Rouge in Paris under the stage name Le Pétomane ("The Mad Farter") and eventually formed his own traveling show. With his amazing butt, this gas master could imitate animals, play melodies on small wind instruments, and even blow out a small flame from yards away. He is also said to have re-created the sounds of the legendary San Francisco earthquake of 1906—completely in farts.

A Field Guide to Flatulence

Farts come in a load of sounds, sizes, and smells. Here are some of the most popular butt expressions.

- **The Trouser Cough.** This short, odorless butt chuckle can be covered up by coughing.

- **The Duck Mallet.** This noisy, occasionally stinky, little fart sounds like the quack of a duck—a tough one to explain away.

- **The Butt Trumpet.** A soaring note that sounds just like a little guy in your butt playing his heart out on a trumpet.

- **The SBD (Silent-But-Deadly).** This room-clearing fart is the source of much finger pointing because it's so stealthy, yet so disgusting.

- **The Ripper.** The noisiest of all, this revolting fart sounds like someone set off wet fireworks in his pants, and smells like he pooped in his shoes.

How to Tame a Beastly Burp

There's no better way to pass time on a car trip than to burp out some of your favorite tunes or to belch out the alphabet. But there are other times—like in the middle of an oral report or at the end of dinner at a *fahncy* restaurant—when it *isn't* so cool to let a burp rip. Here's how to put a cork in it when you have to.

The Art of the Burp

The Stealth Burp

The Crowd Pleaser

1 ## Shut it.

By keeping your teeth and lips together, you'll form an enamel-and-flesh barrier against the air that's trying to escape from your stomach.

2 ## Reroute it.

Allow the burp to fully escape through your nostrils before you open your mouth.

> **BE AWARE** • Just because a burp slips out silently through your nose doesn't mean it won't be noticed—if it's a stinky burp, it'll smell just as bad no matter which way it exits.

3 ## Loosen up.

To prevent other burps from bubbling up, loosen a tight waistband. Too much pressure on your abdomen can mess with your stomach's airflow.

4 ## Air on the side of caution.

The more air you swallow, the more burps you'll blow. So avoid fizzy drinks packed with gases. And don't drink through straws, because you're mostly sucking in air.

The BCS (Burp Classification System)

Some burps are just garden-variety gross, but some are downright disgusting. Here's a brief overview of some common varieties.

- **The Puffer Fish.** This mostly silent, but often smelly, burp escapes in a big gust that puffs out the cheeks and leaks out through the nose.

- **The Door Buzzer.** This brief, odorless burp is usually involuntary and can be identified by its buzzing sound.

- **The Jazz Singer.** Usually done on purpose, often with the aid of soda, this classic burp can change pitch and go on forever. It can be heard in displays of burp-talking.

- **The Creature from the Deep.** A deep, disgusting belch, this out-of-control monster not only sounds like you might be throwing up, it also smells like a nightmare version of your recent meal.

How to Cope with B.O.

P-U! B.O., aka bromhidrosis, is no joke, especially when you can almost see the crazy stink waves floating off your friend. So how do you deal when the air you're breathing is a nasty combo of sweat socks, sour milk, and rotten eggs? Take a whiff of these solutions.

1 Don't blow it.

The best way to avoid another person's body odor is by moving out of his line of stench. If you're outside, make sure you're standing upwind from your foul pal, so his fragrance doesn't gust directly at you. If you're indoors, open the window for a blast of fresh air and make sure he's not in front of it.

2 Fight odor with odor.

If you know your bud's a stinker, dab a drop of perfume or cologne under your nostrils (or just wear it!), so you're smelling *you* instead of Reeky McArmpit. You can also arm yourself with peppermint-flavored gum or hard candy to distract the smell cells in your nose. But if you're caught off guard, you may have to use a more basic means of survival: make a fist and place it under your nostrils to physically block the swamp gas oozing off your friend.

FAST FACT • The smell receptors in your nose quickly get exhausted by strong odors. After only a few minutes of exposure, your nose should stop detecting the stench.

③ Suggest a shower.

Sometimes bad smells happen to good people. Why? Because bacteria living on a person's skin break down pheromones, which are the chemicals produced by specialized sweat glands. And if a person has a lot of pheromones and/or a lot of bacteria, they'll have "a lot" of smell, too. Fortunately, soapy water is bacteria's kryptonite! So the next time you're playing sports with a friend who has a B.O. problem, try to clue him in. Say something like, "Hey, I'm going to hit the showers before we go over to Nick's house. Since you'll probably want one, too, I'll meet you there."

④ Lather up.

But what can you do in an emergency—like when you're at school and showering isn't an option? Just remember that soap is bacteria's mortal enemy. And any enemy of your enemy is your friend! So grab a wet paper towel and soap it up, then slip into a bathroom stall and rub it against your pits, neck, and back to kill the stink-causing bacteria once and for all!

Smelly Feet: The B.O. from Down Below

If your family runs screaming for the air freshener when you take off your shoes, you have a case of stink foot. It develops in an unusually hot, steamy, and poorly ventilated climate: your shoes. Since bacteria love those sweaty conditions, they happily munch on the dead skin cells and oils your feet produce, resulting in the release of a nasty foot funk.

If you want less stinky feet, try wearing socks made of materials that wick away moisture and canvas or leather shoes to give your feet room to breathe. Also, sprinkle some drying foot powder into your sneaks.

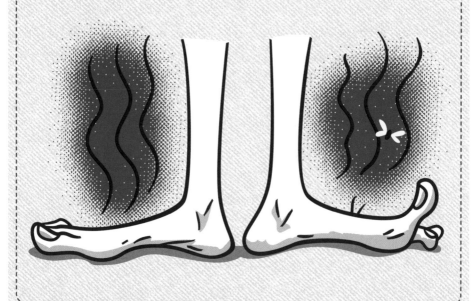

How to Get Rid of a Pimple

Yesterday that red spot next to your nose looked like it might be a mild case of windburn, but today it looks like a cottage-cheese volcano sprouting out of your skin. It's a massive ZIT! Here's how to manage a monster pimple before it becomes a monster headache.

1 Scrub your mug.

Pimples are caused by blockages in your pores, tiny holes in your skin. Each pore is home to a hair follicle and sebaceous glands that produce oil. Sometimes, the oil that normally drains out of the pores can get trapped, creating a buffet for the bacteria hanging out on your skin. To keep your skin from being a bacterial chowhouse, wash it twice a day (in the morning and before bed).

2 Use soft soap.

Just like you wouldn't polish silver with sandpaper, you don't want to anger your skin by cleaning it with an irritating soap. So when washing your face, pick a soap that's unscented and hypoallergenic. (And if you're washing your face twice a day and you're still seeing big flare-ups, it's either time to try a new product or to seek professional help—a dermatologist!)

> **BE AWARE** • Your hands are covered in bacteria and dirt, so unless you've just washed them, keep them away from your face. And *never* squeeze or poke a pimple—you might rupture the clogged pore and make it worse.

Acne: A Spotter's Guide

- **Blackhead.** A blocked hair follicle that is open at the skin's surface. When the gunk inside is exposed to air, it turns black.

- **Whitehead.** A blocked hair follicle that is trapped beneath the surface of the skin and looks like a white spot.

- **Pimple or zit.** A large, red, ruin-your-day bump forms when there's a break in the wall of the hair follicle. Because white blood cells rush in to heal it, you'll eventually see a pus-filled tip.

Shrink (z)it.

To reduce a pimple's swelling and redness, put an ice cube on your mini volcano after washing your face. This should make the pimple less visible. Or, try soaking a washcloth in warm water, then holding it on your zit for a couple of minutes. The heat may help open up your pores and reduce the swelling.

Diagram of a Pimple

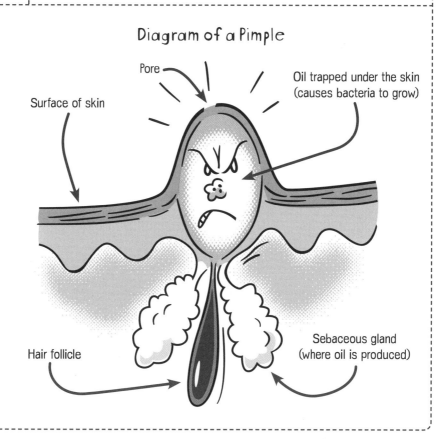

Pore

Oil trapped under the skin
(causes bacteria to grow)

Surface of skin

Hair follicle

Sebaceous gland
(where oil is produced)

Zit Myths Debunked

Just as scientists have confirmed
that acne isn't contagious,
here are some other common
pimple legends.

- **The more you wash, the
  fewer zits you'll get.**
  Washing your face removes
  excess oil and dirt, but
  scrubbing too much or too hard can irritate the skin and dry
  it out, making it more likely to break out.

- **Stress causes pimples.** Hormones (which *can* cause
  pimples—just ask any teenager) are released in small
  amounts during periods of stress, but not enough to cause
  acne. Although as anyone who's had a zit knows, the zit
  itself can cause stress!

- **Zits are caused by eating chocolate, greasy
  foods, and anything that tastes good.** Research
  shows that what we eat does not cause zits, though it sure
  seems like a steady diet of junk food should make it worse....

How to Handle an Oozing Wound

Whether you slid into second base or slipped on the street, you skillfully turned your knee into hamburger meat. Now's the time to do something about it—before that oozing sore becomes infected and you start leaving a trail of slime behind you, slugger.

1 Clean it.

Hold that de-skinned body part under cold running water, then use soap and a washcloth to gently clean the surrounding area.

2 Keep it covered.

Wounds heal nearly twice as fast and are less likely to scar if they're covered and kept germ-free. So after you clean the gash, cover it with an adhesive bandage and change that crusty covering daily until healed. And no show-and-tell for your friends!

3 Get rid of the pus.

When a wound becomes infected, your body sends out white blood cells to fight the infection. Pus—the yellowish-white goop oozing out of the wound—is a combo of these white blood cells, the germs they kill, and any dead skin cells. Since pus is also germ food, it must be removed: either gently wash it away with soap and water (if on the skin's surface), or coax it out with a washcloth soaked in warm water (if under the skin).

4 Don't scrape the scab.

That scab of yours is clotted, dried blood—your body's homemade Band-Aid. It not only stops the blood from

DON'T

DO

leaking out of you, it also forms a barrier against germy invaders. If you pick that scab before it's ready to fall off, you're just reopening your wound, slowing down the healing process, and putting yourself at risk for an infection. So don't give in to the picking urge, because pickers never heal and healers never pick!

Gangrene: Infected Wounds Gone Bad

If you hold your breath, your face turns red, right? Well, if blood stops flowing to certain parts of your body, your flesh doesn't get the oxygen it needs and it eventually turns black and dies. That delightful effect is called gangrene, and it can happen if a wound gets so infected that the pus can't drain out, stopping blood flow to the area. Luckily, gangrene can be stopped with antibiotics and other medical treatments, including one of the grossest cures ever invented: *maggot therapy.* Doctors place a squirming horde of green bottle fly maggots (see page 80) into the infected wound. Since these maggots eat only rotten meat, they devour the dead and dying flesh but leave the healthy bits alone. Once they've cleaned out the wound, the maggots are removed. And considering the smell, that might be a good time to start holding your breath!

How to Wrestle a Wart

No witch costume is complete without adding a wart. But what about when it's *not* Halloween and you're not trying to look like a witch? Well, when a wart crops up on your skin, it sure can make you *feel* like a witch. Though these aren't magic potions, the following tips will help your wart disappear.

1 **Don't scratch.**

Common warts are gnarly growths in the outer layers of your skin caused by a virus that is spread by contact. So even though Mount Wartsuvius might itch, don't scratch it. You'll just get the virus under your fingernails, and from there you could spread it to other parts of your body, like your hands, elbows, knees, and feet.

> **FAST FACT •** A wart on the sole of your foot is called a plantar wart, and it's the only kind of wart that's really painful. One of these warts can feel like you've got a pebble permanently stuck in your shoe.

❷ Stay dry.

Like mushrooms, warts love to grow in moist, wet places. So always completely dry off after you go swimming or take a shower, making sure to wipe the spaces between your toes and other crevices with the towel. If you already have a wart, use a clean towel the next time, so you don't accidentally spread the old wart to a new place!

❸ Wage wart war.

Sometimes warts will just go away on their own. But if you have one that insists on hanging around, there are medicines you can use and doctors you can see. There are also all sorts of home remedies out there that—who knows—might actually work! Just ask a parent before

venturing into the kitchen (or office supply drawer) to try one of these wart busters.

- **Apply banana peels.** The potassium in the banana peel supposedly kills the virus.
- **Pour on apple cider vinegar.** The acid in the vinegar is supposed to burn the wart away.
- **Duct tape it.** The chemicals in duct tape are believed to kill the virus. Or the wart just decides it doesn't want to con"duct" its business this way.

Real or Ridiculous?

There are a lot of wacky wart ideas out there! Can you tell which beliefs are real and which are ridiculous?

a. You can get warts from touching a frog or toad.

b. Warts put down roots deep into your bones.

c. A wart can last for years.

d. Warts can grow on your face.

e. You can get warts under your nails.

Answers: a. and b. are ridiculous.

CHAPTER 2

Home

How to Deal with Gross Food

Holy plop on a plate! A weapon of mass digestive destruction now sits in front of you and you've been told to "Eat up!" Here are some tricks to help you deal when the meal does *not* appeal.

TRICK #1: The Plate-to-Napkin Transfer

Unless you want to fork lift this so-called food into your mouth, it's time to sweep those vicious vittles off your plate and into your napkin.

1 Stage a distraction.

To draw attention away from yourself, try one of these lines.

- "Mom, is that a tarantula on the wall behind you?"
- "I dropped a twenty under the table—anyone see it?"
- "People with big brains can't completely cover their faces with both hands. See if *you* can…"
- "Bet you can't describe the inside of your eyelids."

2 Nap(kin) time!

When everyone's distracted, scrape the hurl-burger off the plate and into your napkin, fold the napkin up, and place the bundle in your lap.

3 Dispose of the evidence.

Barf Burrito in hand, excuse yourself to go to the bathroom. Flush the contents of the napkin—but not the drain-clogging napkin itself—down the toilet. Or if you have huge pockets, wait to chuck it into some distant trash can (where the chef won't discover it) later!

Mastering the Plate-to-Napkin Transfer

STEP 1
Casually bring napkin up to plate.

STEP 2
Carefully place fork on plate.

STEP 3
Slide food into napkin with fork.

STEP 4
Wrap napkin up and prepare to toss it away.

TRICK #2: The Mouth-to-Napkin Transfer

Put your game face on. This tough trick involves holding the chow in your mouth before blowing it into that handy dandy napkin.

1 Take a bite.

To slide the food in your mouth without gagging, blow air out your nose in short, quick bursts. Think *breathing*, not chewing.

2 Wipe the food away.

Look for your moment. (Hint: It's not when all eyes are on you!) When everyone's distracted, pretend to wipe your lips with the napkin while spitting the food into it. Then wrap up that napkin like a present to give to the garbage can!

> **BE AWARE** • Feeding a dog from the dinner table is not recommended. A lot of human food (onions and avocados, for instance) can make dogs sick, which could lead to a super-gross outcome: you, cleaning up dog vomit or diarrhea off the living room rug.

Packed with Vitamins...and Rat Hair

That jumbo jar of creamy peanut butter seems so pure—it's "sealed for your protection," right? In fact, the U.S. government allows a certain amount of insect parts, rat fur, maggots, and mold in packaged foods. Here's what you might come across in some very common foods.

- **Chocolate:** Up to 60 insect parts and 1 rodent hair per ¼ pound (113 grams)

- **Pasta:** Up to 225 insect parts or 4 rodent hairs per ½ pound (230 grams)

- **Peanut butter:** Up to 30 insect fragments or 1 rodent hair per ¼ pound (113 grams)

- **Potato chips:** Up to 6 percent of the chips can be from rotten potatoes

- **Pizza sauce:** Up to 30 fly eggs or 15 fly eggs and 1 maggot or 2 entire maggots per ¼ pound (113 grams)

How to Avoid Old Food in the Fridge

Eating food spoiled by bacteria or mold can make you hurl, give you the squirts, or worse. Here's how to avoid the Chunky Milk and Furry Food in your fridge.

1 ## Use your Smell-O-Meter.

Checking the expiration date is always your first line of defense against bacteria lurking in liquids. But for drinks that *don't* have a date, take a whiff to see if it smells sour (which means bacteria are digesting the

What Is Mold?

Mold is a fungus that reproduces by sending out microscopic spores that travel through the air until they reach food and start growing a new colony. To digest food, molds make enzymes that make people sick, so *never* eat food that's furry. (As if you would!)

juice and secreting their sour-smelling enzymes). Your nose has more than five million receptors that will tell you if it's bad with one whiff.

2 Spot the dots.

When you're dealing with food like a sandwich or leftovers, toss anything with small fuzzy white dots—the first signs that mold has set up shop.

3 Seal the spores.

If your food has a full-on furry coat of mold, put it in a bag and seal it tightly before throwing away. The fur means that mold spores are present, and you'll want to keep them contained—otherwise, they'll turn your kitchen into a Mold Metropolis!

How to Tell if There's a Mouse in Your House

Did you hear a scratching sound? Or a high-pitched squeak? Did you see a fast moving shadow out of the corner of your eye? Uh-oh....Time to start looking for some telltale signs of your mouse-guest.

1 Snoop for poop.

One mouse can drop up to 9,000 poop pellets—tiny black sausages with pointy ends—in just six months. You'll find these mini-logs near walls, inside kitchen cabinets, and anywhere a mouse feeds.

2 Check for holes.

Mice *love* grains and nuts, so they often head right for the cereal in your pantry. Check for ragged holes in bottoms of boxes and bags, and discard anything they've chomped. Why? Mice tend to poop and pee while they eat.

③ Watch for pet freak-outs.

With their amazing senses of smell, dogs and cats are often the first to know you've got mice. If your pet suddenly starts paying a lot of attention to the space under the dishwasher or behind the fridge, that's probably where your new roommate is chilling out.

BE AWARE • The Black Death, or bubonic plague, is a disease carried by fleas living on rodents, like mice. An outbreak that peaked in 1348 killed nearly half the human population of Europe, and it's still around today! Your chances of catching it are very slim, but if you did catch it, a round of antibiotics would wipe it out.

How to Scoop Dog Poop

Dog poop is stinky, mushy, and full of bacteria—and nothing can ruin a perfectly nice day like stepping into a steaming heap of the stuff. That's probably why there are laws requiring dog owners to scoop their pup's poop or face a fine! Here's how to survive doing your doo-ty.

1 Get a poop-proof bag.

Plastic grocery and produce bags make great pooper scoopers. But make sure the bag is hole-free *before* you head out on poop patrol. To test the bag, blow it up with air—you'll be able to tell right away if there are any breaks or tears.

2 Pop on your poop mitten.

Before you stoop to scoop the pile of poop, place the bag over the lucky hand that's about to make the grab. Unfold the bag as far as possible—this will protect your forearm from any poop morsels that accidentally escape.

3 Hold your breath.

Before bending down to pluck the dog dookie from the ground, take a breath of fresh air. If you don't, the smell down in Pooptown could make you spew chunks on top of the pile—making an awful chore far worse.

4 Doo the doggie bag.

Here's how to grab your dog's poo in five easy steps:

STEP 1
Place a bag over one hand.

STEP 2
Grab the poo.

STEP 3
Invert the bag with your other hand.

STEP 4
Seal the bag (but not with a kiss)!

STEP 5
Dispose of the poo in a proper waste receptacle. It is now safe to breathe again.

5 Bust out the hose.

If the poop in question is diarrhea, don't even try to pick it up—there's no good way to pick up poop that looks like it's gone through a blender. If you are faced with liquid leavings, rinse the poo puddle away using a lawn hose or watering can.

FAST FACT • The nearly 400 million dogs in the world squeeze out enough poop to fill almost 83,000 Olympic-sized swimming pools every year.

"How Nice to Smell You Again!" Gross Dog Behavior

Here are some examples of what passes for good manners in the dog world.

- **Sniffing puddles of pee.** Dogs do this to keep up with their fellow dogs' comings and goings.

- **Smelling and licking each other's butts.** Dogs recognize each other by the smell and taste of their poop and pee.

- **Peeing on everything.** It's how dogs say, "I was here!"

- **Rolling around in dead animals or in poop.** Dogs' hunting instincts make them want to cover their own odor with a stronger smell so they can sneak up on prey.

- **Eating cat poop.** Dogs like cat logs because they're rich in protein.

How to Manage Your Cat's Hairballs

Hack! Hack! Hack! There's that sound again: either your cat is trying to cough up an elephant...or that's a big fat hairball working its way out. Here's how to keep Tabby from coughing up slimy, stinky hair wads all over the house.

1 Brush, brush, brush.

When kitty cleans her coat from paws to butt, she licks up loose strands of fur, causing hairballs to form in her stomach. To prevent this, brush her once a day from head to tail, preferably outdoors, with a special cat hair brush or comb (or even a lint roller!).

> **FAST FACT** • An eighteen-year-old woman, fond of eating her hair (a habit called trichophagia), had a 10-pound (4.5 kg), bowling ball–sized hairball surgically removed from her stomach in 2007. No way was she coughing *that* thing up.

② Grease 'er up.

Adding a little petroleum jelly (about the size of your pinky nail) to kitty's Seafood Surprise once a day should help that hairball go slip-sliding right out of your cat. If your cat isn't a fan of the PJ mystery mush, buy a flavored, over-the-counter remedy at the pet store.

③ Call the doctor.

If you've tried these hairball treatments but Tabby's still hacking up hair, it's time to call the vet. The problem might be something more serious than a hair clog.

How to Stop an Overflowing Toilet

Even light plumbing is a job for adults. But if you're home alone and the toilet water starts rising to the top of the bowl after you flush, you may have to plunge into action. Here's how to unclog the toilet and keep the SS *Chocolate Banana* and the rest of the Brown Armada from setting sail for the living room.

1 Grab the plunger.

Now is the time to use that stick with the funny rubber thing on the end. Use the rubber end of the plunger to bat away any floaters in the water, like poop or toilet paper. Then use it to cover the hole at the bottom of the bowl. Make sure the plunger is firmly in place before you start plugging away, or you may get a mud bath!

2 Push and pull.

Push the plunger handle down, then pull it back up, making sure the plunger is always snugly over the hole.

As you move up and down, you should feel a resistance building—this means it's working. Keep pumping the plunger until the clog gives way, which will sound like a giant whoosh. It is now safe to flush any remaining trouser gravy.

3 ## Disinfect your tools.

Now that you're done, you'll want to clean your plunger. Keep it in the toilet bowl and flush once more so the water is clear. Then pour in some toilet bowl cleaner and swish the plunger around, getting it nice and soapy. Flush again, and use the new water to clean the soap off of the plunger. Your plunger is now ready for the next clog.

Take the Plunge

Cover the hole with the plunger. Push the plunger down and pull it back up until the clog gives way.

And don't forget to disinfect!

The World's Grossest Jobs

Think it's gross unclogging a backed-up toilet? Imagine having one of these jobs.

- **Breath odor evaluator.** In order to make sure breath mints and mouthwash actually work, someone has to smell the "before" breath and the "after" breath.

- **Porta-potty cleaner.** This person not only scrubs down those portable plastic toilets but also sucks out their liquid contents with a powerful vacuum.

- **Bat poop collector.** Much grosser than collecting stamps, this collector crawls through caves scraping up the poop of millions of bats. Bat poop (guano) is used to make garden fertilizer and gunpowder.

- **Sewage lift pump repair-person.** Toilet waste goes to a sewage processing plant. When that plant's lift pump breaks, the repair-person puts on diving gear and swims into a tank of poop and pee to bring the pump to the surface to be fixed.

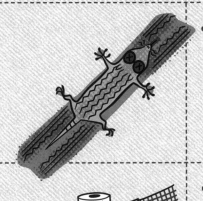

- **Roadkill cleaner.** All those squished raccoons, squirrels, deer, and other animals don't clean themselves off the road!

- **Worm farmer.** Animal poop can't be used as garden fertilizer until it has been eaten and pooped out again by billions of worms—all cared for (and fed tons and tons of poop) by the worm farmer.

How to Cope with a Fly Infestation

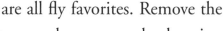

As you sit down to lunch, a housefly pulls a loop-the-loop and makes a perfect landing on your PB&J. "At least it's not a bee," you think, shooing it away. *Well, not really*: Sure, flies won't sting you, but they do hang out in dog poop and roadkill all day. Not exactly appetizing dinner guests. Here's how to keep flies from getting comfortable in your kitchen.

1 Seal the trash.

Nothing screams "Come on in!" to a fly like an open garbage can: meat scraps, curdled milk, and rotten fruit are all fly favorites. Remove the welcome mat by keeping the lid on. Also, rinse food containers before tossing them in the recycle bin.

② Clean the kitty litter.

To a fly, poop smells and tastes like the finest of chocolates. So if you have a cat, clean its litter-box often, and tightly seal any poo-filled garbage bags.

FAST FACT • Since flies can only eat liquids, they spit on their food, wait for chemicals in the saliva to turn it into a goopy puddle, and then suck it all in. Bon appétit!

③ Scout the source.

Do a poop and dead animal check in the backyard. See a buzzing cloud of flies? This usually means there's a pile of butt lumber or an ex-chipmunk nearby. A

rotting carcass is like an invitation to a fly party. If you discover a dead animal, ask an adult to take it to its final resting place—far away from your home!

The Life Cycle of the Housefly

Our story begins on a beautiful, warm spring day when a female housefly lays her eggs in a welcoming pile of fresh poop...

PHASE 1
After two flies mate, the mom flies off and lays 500 eggs in batches of 75 to 100 on dead animals, garbage, or piles of poop.

PHASE 2
Less than a day later, hungry little maggots hatch from the eggs and start eating.

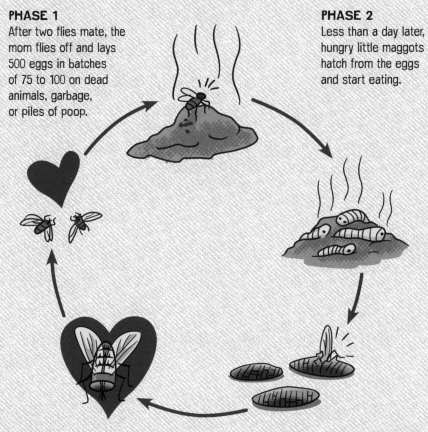

PHASE 4
After two to six days, having completed their amazing transformation, full-grown flies burst from the pupae and go off in search of their soul mates!

PHASE 3
About a week after that, well-fed maggots transform into pupae (imagine hard, reddish-brown, pill-shaped containers).

CHAPTER 3

School

How to Navigate the School Bathroom

Among its smells, sights, and sounds, the bathroom at school can seem like a chamber (pot) of horrors. And having to visit that nasty place can feel more punishing than being sent to the principal's office. But, dude, when you've gotta go, you've gotta go, so here's how to do your private business in a public toilet.

① Use the first stall.

Here's a little secret: whether you need to go number one or number two, the best call is to pick door number one! Most people think everyone uses the first stall, so they head to the farthest stall, assuming it'll be cleaner. Wrong! Your best bet for a clean toilet is to go for the one nearest the door.

② Use the toe-flip.

You need to use a public toilet, but the seat and/or lid is down. Obviously, you *don't* want to put your fingers near where other people's heinies hover, but shouting "OPEN SESAME" won't work. Here's how to open that bowl with very little hand-to-seat contact.

1. Balance on one leg, ninja-style.
2. With the lifted leg, catch the edge of the lid (or the seat) with the toe of your shoe.
3. Now give it a good flip.

The Toilet Toe-flip

STEP 1
Balance on one leg.

STEP 2
Lift the lid with your toe.

STEP 3
Flip the lid.

Urine Says a Lot About You

Pay attention to your pee. It could be trying to tell you something!

Hey, you're not drinking enough water!

- **It's dark yellow.** Normally, pee is pale yellow, but if you haven't been drinking enough water, your kidneys hold onto whatever water they can, rather than passing it through—making your pee more concentrated and really yellow.

- **It's bright yellow, or even orange.** Taking certain medications and vitamins (especially too much vitamin B) can make your pee look fluorescent yellow.

- **It's reddish.** If you've just eaten blackberries, rhubarb, or beets, don't be alarmed by this colorful outcome.

- **It smells like rotten eggs.** Did you just eat asparagus? Then your pee is about to get stinky. Fast. (You may not notice; a lot of people can't actually detect this smell in pee.)

③ Protect the throne.

Before setting cheeks to seat, wipe away any obvious splatter with TP. But what about microscopic grossness? Do you need to worry about that? Surprisingly, that mighty throne isn't the worst offender in the Kingdom of Crud—phone receivers are far germier! Still, to ease your mind (and bum), make yourself a fanny shield before doing your royal doo-ty. Yank off enough toilet paper to cover each side of the seat. Then, place the TP on the left and right sides of the seat.

> **BE AWARE •** The dirtiest surfaces in public bathrooms are the flushers and stall handles because they're what people touch after they take care of their business but before they wash their hands.

④ Do the crouch.

If the stall looks like it was sprayed with a hose full of yuck, you may not even want to sit on a TP-lined seat. This is when the crouch comes in handy. Back up to the toilet, and place your feet as far apart as possible (to help keep your balance). Then lower your butt until it's hovering just above the seat, and fire away.

Poopisms

Whether you cheer it or fear it, one thing's for certain: poop happens. As we've heard time and time again, everybody poops. But funnily enough, not everybody calls it by the same name. Here are some other ways to describe the brown bomber.

• **Pooping**	Build a Log Cabin, Drop the Kids off at the Pool, Pinch a Loaf, Take a Dump
• **Poop**	Brown Bananas, Butt Biscuits, Butt Links, Butt Mud, Captain's Log, Chocolate Chunks, Dookie (or Dook), Logs, Number Two, Toilet Snakes, Turds
• **Diarrhea**	Muddy Waters, The Runs, The Squirts

How to Deal with the Gum Under Your Desk

You're concentrating like crazy on that test in front of you. Your fidgety right leg is bouncing under the desk when—AHHHHH!—it touches something soft and sticky. Here's what to do if you get gummed.

1 ### Wrap it up.

Never use your bare hands to remove ABC (Already Been Chewed) gum. No matter how fossilized it seems to be, old gum is still crawl-ing with germs. Instead, use a plastic bag or folded-up piece of notebook paper to pluck off the gum. And if there are bits of gum that won't budge, press little pieces of paper over 'em to keep your pants from getting stuck.

> **FAST FACT** • While most bacteria and viruses need moisture to survive, some germs can live in a piece of ABC gum for up to a year.

2 Pry it off.

When the gum is really hard, you'll need to make a wedge to help you lift it off. Fold a piece of notebook paper into eighths, until it's a thick rectangle. Insert the edge of this rectangular wedge between the gum and the desk, and use it to pry the crusty old nugget off.

3 Mind your knees.

If you can't remove the gum before class starts or if the gum just won't budge, try to practice your freeze-frame skills. One wild knee bounce and you could wind up with jeans full of extra-sticky gum cooties. So do your best to keep your legs grounded!

The Great Gum Walls of America

Chew on this: there are places in the United States—some are even tourist attractions!—where it's A-OK to stick your ABC gum.

- **Bubblegum Alley** *(San Luis Obispo, California)*. First gummed in the 1940s or 1950s by local college students who wrote their initials and created pictures with gum. Today, layers of gum cover the walls on both sides of the alley, but the precise number of master"pieces" in the alley gallery remains unknown!

- **Market Theater Gum Wall** *(Seattle, Washington)*. In 1993, lines of people waiting to get into the theater near Pike Place Market to see comedy shows started leaving their wads behind. Now the wall is completely covered in a rainbow of old gum chunks. Colorful? Yes. Tasteful? No.

When Your Bubble Bursts...on You!

One minute you're blowing a bubble of world-record proportion. The next—disaster! You're now in the running to become the world's biggest gummy bear. When your gum goes "pop" and your new shirt gets fizzed, try this method to get the sticky stuff out.

1. Place the shirt in the freezer.

2. After two hours, remove the shirt and use a butter knife (or a toothbrush if your shirt is silk, satin, or some other delicate fabric) to scrape off the gum, which should now be brittle.

3. Wash your shirt and, *voilà*, goodbye gum!

How to Survive Lice

Lots of things get passed around in class, including really gross stuff—like lice. Those annoying little bugs set up base camp on your scalp and have a party until you get rid of them. Here's how to protect your noggin against these blood-grubbing little vampires.

1 Check your head.

You can tell if your scalp feels dry and itchy, but unless you have eyes in the back of your skull, it's hard to do a full head scan by yourself. So ask an adult to check if you've got scalp company. Here's how to catch sight of the lice.

- **Stand under a very bright light.** Lice are hard to see. They're small—about the size of a sesame seed—they change color from tan to dark brown to match the hair they live in, and they move fast.

- **Look in a few different spots.** Lice move away from light, so you may have to quickly check several spots to see one before it scurries away.

- **Part the hair and look near the scalp.** Lice attach their eggs (nits) to the bottoms of hair shafts with their super-sticky saliva. The nits can be white or yellow.

BE AWARE • Lice cannot fly or jump, but they're great crawlers. They can scramble directly from one juicy scalp to the next when you're in close contact with others. They also hang out on hats, brushes, and anything else that touches people's heads.

2 Comb 'em out.

The best way to get rid of lice is to have an adult scrape them from your hair with a stainless steel lice comb— a special comb with teeth that are *really* close together. Here's how to make the comb work for you.

1. Slather your hair in white hair conditioner—this will help you get the comb through your hair *and* help you see any lice or nits.

2. Insert the comb into the hair right next to the scalp, then slowly pull it out. Wipe the gobs of conditioner and any critters or eggs you comb out onto a paper towel.

3. Repeat until every single hair has been combed from end to end and you no longer see any lice or nits in the conditioner.

4. Place the lice-covered paper towels into a garbage bag, tie it off, and put it out with the trash.

3 Scrubba, scrubba, scrubba!

After delousing, wash any clothes, sheets, and towels you've used within the last two days in very hot water. Then pop these items in the dryer and turn the heat on high for at least thirty minutes for some fried lice!

A Day in the Life of a Louse

- **6:00 a.m.** Breakfast time! Louise Louse grabs your scalp with her mouth claws and sinks tiny tubes (stylets) into your blood vessels for a drink. You don't feel a thing.

- **7:30 a.m.** Mrs. Louse spits onto one of your hair shafts. Then she attaches 10 eggs to the sticky gob of saliva.

- **9:00 a.m.** You step into the shower. Mrs. Louse holds her breath and wraps all six of her claw-tipped legs around a hair to keep from being swept away.

- **12:00 p.m.** Lunch—more (of your) blood!

- **2:30 p.m.** Crawling past some eggs she stuck to your hair last week, Mrs. Louse is pleased to see that itsy-bitsy newborn lice (nymphs) are hatching.

- **4:00 p.m.** Snack—blood again!

- **6:30 p.m.** Mrs. Louse watches proudly as her five-day-old nymphs perfect their blood-sucking skills on your scalp. In four days, they'll be all grown-up!

- **9:30 p.m.** You go to bed and all the lice move around to avoid getting squashed on your pillow.

- **10:00 p.m.** Dinnertime—blood pudding!

- **1:30 a.m.** Looking for a new place to lay some eggs, Mrs. Louse takes a stroll through your eyebrows as you sleep.

- **3:00 a.m.** Mrs. Louse has a quick snack of blood before heading out to explore your pillow with some friends.

- **5:30 a.m.** All aboard your head, ready for a new day!

How to Prevent Pinkeye

The glowing red eyes of your class-mates may mean they've all become ZOMBIES! Or they've caught the dreaded pinkeye, an eye infection that can spread like wildfire around  a school. Here's how to keep the pink out of *your* eyes.

1 Don't touch.

When you hang out with someone who's got pinkeye, keep your hands away from your face—even if you just washed them (you may not be aware that you've touched your friend or her belongings). Pinkeye germs are ultra-contagious! If you *really* need to rub your eyes, use your forearm or pull your sleeve over your hand before you rub.

FAST FACT • Pinkeye can be viral or bacterial. The bacterial kind produces a gross, thick, greenish-yellowish fluid.

❷ Respect(acle) your eyes.

Trying on a friend's sunglasses is like giving germs a ferry ride from his eyes to yours and back again, which is why you should never swap specs. Or swim goggles, ski masks, SCUBA masks, 3-D glasses…

❸ Change your pillowcase.

If you do catch pinkeye, don't stress. It usually clears up on its own in three to fourteen days. To make sure you don't re-infect your eye, or infect your good eye, replace your pillowcase before going to bed every night until the infection's gone. (Change your towels daily, too!)

Keep the Pink-Eyed Monster Away

DON'T: Rub your eyes.   **DO:** Wash your hands.

How to Handle the Water Fountain

You're so thirsty you think you might faint, when you spot an oasis—a water fountain! But before you slurp up its offerings, just remember that within that shiny bubbler some serious slime could be lurking. Here's how to avoid gargling grossness.

1 Be picky.

The pressure! The low water pressure! If the water doesn't spray up very high no matter how hard you press the button, avoid wrapping your lips around the germy spigot, and find another source. When you *do* find a less disgusting water fountain…

2 Handle with care.

Think twice before touching the handle with your bare hand. The knob can carry more cooties than a wadded up snot rag! So grab the handle with your sleeve or the hem of your T-shirt.

3 Use the five-second rule.

Let the water run for a solid five seconds before you bend down for a sip. Doing this will wash away any (wet) germs the last person dribbled back into the spigot.

FAST FACT • The drinking fountain was invented by plumber Luther Haws in 1906, after he saw school children in Berkeley, California, drinking from the same tin cup attached to the school's faucet. And you thought the fountain at your school was a surefire way to spread germs!

How to Wrestle Ringworm

Just like the chickpea, which is neither a chick nor a pea, ringworm is neither a ring nor a worm. But what ringworm *is* is one of the itchiest, most contagious skin infections you can catch at school! Spreading through skin-to-skin contact, it often starts as a scaly irritated patch, but can morph into a circular rash that looks like a thin, red worm curled up in a ring just under your skin. Here's how to fend off this itchy fungus.

1 Ban bare feet.

Ringworm fungus loves to hang out in warm, steamy places, just waiting for a chance to spread to someone's skin or scalp. This is why you should wear shoes, sandals, or flip-flops in wet places where people walk around barefoot: gyms, locker rooms, and swimming pools. It's also why you should change your socks every day—you don't want your socks to become fungus farms!

❷ Opt for air-drying.

A damp towel is the perfect home for ringworm (and zillions of other creepy fungi), so use paper towels, the air dryer, or even the back of your pants to dry your hands.

> **FAST FACT** • Ringworm can survive in a dirty sock or towel for up to eighteen months!

❸ Wash your kicks.

To keep ringworm from growing in your sneakers, pop them into the washer (by themselves and on the hottest setting), then into the dryer (or air out in direct sunlight for an entire day) once a month.

Fungi or Fun Guy?

Warm, steamy places, like your sweaty shoes, are havens for fungi.

Dry your kicks in direct sunlight to keep 'em fungi free.

Worms That Make You Squirm

Ringworm may really be a fungus, but there are plenty of *actual* worms to be grossed out by. Here are four notorious members of the parasitic worm gang.

- **Tapeworm.** This ultra-long worm grows in the intestines of people and animals and can reach lengths of up to 50 feet (15 meters) and live for twenty years.

- **Pinworm.** These small worms (about the size of a rice grain) usually grow in the intestines of children. Eggs are pooped out and spread when people scratch their butts (squirmy pinworms cause itching!) and touch stuff around the house.

- **Ascaris.** This nasty worm grows up to 20 inches (50 cm) long in a person's intestines. The adult females can lay hundreds of thousands of eggs per day, leading to a gigantic squirming family of worms inside a person's body.

- **Guinea Worm.** The eggs of this worm enter a person's body through contaminated drinking water. The young worms travel through the body to the skin of the lower legs, where they continue to grow. At adulthood, the tip of the worm pokes out of the skin through a painful blister.

CHAPTER 4

The Wild Kingdom

How to Avoid Bird Poop

It's hot, wet, smelly, and *literally* out of the blue. If you've ever gotten paint-balled with bird poop, you know what it's like to have the liquid remains of some bird's last worm right there on your shirt (or maybe even in your hair!). G to the R to the OSS! Here are some tips to avoid being a bird potty.

1 Avoid favorite bird hangouts.

Birds are more likely to do their business while perched rather than flying. Trees, building ledges, and telephone wires are all popular bird hangouts. So it's best to avoid standing under places where birds of a feather flock together.

2 Spot the splatter.

Though you might think the best way to find evidence of birds is to scan up above, any detective worth his gumshoe will tell you to also look down. Do you see poop splatter? One or two splats o' poo probably isn't a big deal. But if you can play connect-the-dots with birdie blobs, you just might be in the center of a bird-poop bull's-eye. Now RUN!

BE AWARE • Bird poop that piles up in large amounts can contain fungi and bacteria that can make you sick—even poop that's been lying around for a while. So always wash your hands after touching bird poop, even if it's really old.

❸ De-turd.

Here's how to remove the poop if a bird butt-bombs you.

1. Let the poop dry out. If you try to wipe up fresh bird dookie, you will only make the mess bigger and grind it deeper into the fabric.

2. After the poop is completely dry, use a paper towel to pull it off in clumps. Any bits left clinging to the clothing should be scraped off with an old toothbrush. Go from the edge of the stain inward so you don't spread the poop. Oh, and that toothbrush? It should *never* be used for teeth again.

3. Using a sponge and warm, soapy water, wipe down any chalky poop dust left on your clothes. Now your clothes are ready for a trip through the wash.

FAST FACT • Because birds pee, poop, and lay eggs through the same hole (the cloaca, the Latin word for "sewer"), bird poop is actually a pee/poop combo platter.

Eye-popping Animal Poops

Some animal poop arrives in weird colors, some comes in huge quantities, and some is used in unexpected ways. Here are some of nature's most astonishing poops.

- **Hyena poop.** A hyena's turds are bone-white, just like the bones the hyena loves to eat with its powerful jaws and teeth.

- **Elephant poop.** An adult elephant's daily dumps add up to the weight of a ten-year-old boy. And the poop doesn't go to waste—Asian elephant poop is turned into paper products.

- **Koala poop.** A baby koala eats an appetizer of its mother's poop before munching eucalyptus leaves. The bacteria in mom's poop help the little koala digest the tough foliage.

- **Vulture poop.** This giant bird poops on its own feet to keep cool in its desert habitat. And if *that's* not gross enough, a vulture does this while sitting around waiting for animals to die.

How to Get Rid of a Roach

You shuffle into the kitchen for a midnight snack, when—*whoa*! You turn on the light and find yourself in a teeming roach motel! It may seem like a bad dream, but your home has been overtaken by an army of multi-legged, armor-plated creepy crawlers that are scurrying across your floor. Don't just stand there! It's time to take action against these dirty and disgusting intruders.

1 **Get red of them.**

If you're going to wage a War of the Roaches, surprise can be your secret weapon. Turns out roaches can't see red light. Remain invisible to these nocturnal creatures by using a flashlight with a red bulb, or a piece of red paper taped over the lens, while leaving the other lights off. When the roaches come out to party, you can sneak up on them, and they won't know what hit 'em until it's too late!

The Omnivorous Roach

You might think you're open to eating anything and everything, but a roach really does eat everything it can get its hairy legs on. Here are some of its favorite *inedible* delicacies.

• Soap	• Plastic	• Animal fur
• Ink	• Paper	• Animal and roach poop
• Paint	• Clothing	• Other roaches
• Glue	• Wood	• Roach eggs

2 Slide stealthily.

Since roaches are sensitive to small breezes (like the one created by your body as you walk), they'll try to flee as soon as they catch wind of you. So stalk them slowly, and be sure to get between the roaches and any small space, like near the refrigerator or stove (they like dashing under both), or near door frames.

> **FAST FACT** • The American cockroach is one of the fastest land insects in the world. This large roach, about the size of a peanut shell, can run up to 34 mph (54 kph). The human equivalent would be to run 200 mph (320 kph)—as fast as a sports car at top speed!

3 Crush without touching.

Roaches walk through garbage, eat trash, carry diseases, and poop all over the place. And many people have allergic reactions to their poop, spit, and bodies—everything from a rash to full-blown asthma. So it's never a good idea to touch them with your bare hands! When you crush a roach, use an old magazine you don't mind tossing out afterward or the sole of a shoe.

The Dung Beetle:
Poop Lover of the Insect World

What do you think the "dung" in "dung beetle" means? Dung beetles like to hang around near dung? They like to eat dung? They like to live in dung? It's worse than you think—it's all three! Dung beetles love poop more than anything else in the world. With their excellent sense of smell, they can sniff out their favorite meal—a hot, steaming turd soufflé. Some dung beetles even live inside a big pile of poop, while others cling to the hairy butts of various animals, so they can get a steady diet of freshly made poop.

There is also a dung beetle that collects a big round ball of poop—as much as fifty times as big as its body—and rolls it away from the master dump site before another hungry dung beetle can steal it. Then it stashes its poop ball underground, either for eating it or laying eggs in later. As sick as it sounds, we owe these poop-loving insects thanks since they help fertilize the soil and keep more flies from breeding. Still, we don't recommend thanking them with an invitation to dinner!

How to Survive a Skunk Encounter

Imagine getting farted on by the world's largest elephant. Now double that breezy aroma and add rotten eggs and blue cheese to the stench. *That* is what getting sprayed by a skunk smells like. So unless you enjoy the odor of eye-stingingly strong skunk juice, here's how to stay out of the spray's way.

1 Read the skunk signals.

A skunk gives plenty of warning before it blasts away with its butt-mounted stink cannons. It will growl, stomp the ground, fluff its tail, and spit angrily if you get too close. Take a whiff of the hint and get out of there. NOW!

2 High-tail it.

A skunk's tail lifted sky high is a sure sign that he's about to blow. So if you're not already in motion, now is the time to make like diarrhea and run. But don't act startled—skunks only spray when they're scared, so stay calm and walk backward slooowly.

Skunk Cabbage: Smelly Super Plant

Stinky like its namesake, this swamp-loving plant *smells* like the dead—which is why flies and other insects that like to eat and lay their eggs in rotting meat are drawn to it. Besides its mind-bending aroma, it has another amazing ability: the skunk cabbage can generate a lot of heat—as much as 20° F (7° C) above the outdoor temperature, melting away snow and ice to start growing long before other, nicer-smelling plants get a chance.

③ **If you do get sprayed...**

The warm, oily, butt vapor coating your skin will make you smell worse than the lowest form of dumpster sludge. Waste no time getting that Eau de Skunk off your clothes and skin. It's oil-based, which means that it can really soak in. These steps will help slay the spray.

1. In a large bowl, mix together 1 quart (1 liter) white vinegar, ¼ cup (55 grams) baking soda, and 2 teaspoons (10 milliliters) liquid dish soap.

2. Rub half of the concoction into your clothes, then place them in a big bowl or large pot to soak while you take a shower.

3. In the shower, wash your skin with half of the remaining mixture, paying special attention to where the skunk sprayed. Let the potion sit on your skin for two minutes before rinsing. Repeat with the rest of the mixture. Then wash with regular soap.

4. After your shower, toss your contaminated clothes (and nothing else) into the washing machine and wash on the hottest setting.

The Stinkiest Creatures on Earth

Skunks aren't the only members of the animal kingdom with mind-meltingly bad smells. Here are the superstar stinkers of the wild.

- **Tasmanian Devil** (Australia). These tough little dudes are said to smell like the dead! But imagine what kind of scents you'd shoot out your rear if you ate nearly half your body weight in a single meal!

- **Wolverine** (North America and Northern Europe). Also known as "skunk bears," wolverines smear their strong rotten-egg odor everywhere to mark their territory and warn off enemies. Turns out they're relatives of the weasel...are you surprised?

- **Striped polecat** (Africa). Widely considered *the* stinkiest animal on Earth, these animals that look like large skunks produce an odor so strong, you need to be *more* than 10 city blocks away to be out of their stink zone!

How to Remove a Tick

You know that hard, scabby thingamajig on your lower leg? Look at it closely, and you'll see that it has several sets of legs of its own! And it has a head, too…but you probably can't see it because that part of the tick is now burrowing in your flesh. AHHH! And if that's not dizzying enough for you, how 'bout this? While digging into your skin, it's also drinking your blood. Here's how to keep from being the main course on a tick's menu.

1 Grab an adult.

Ticks are tricky creatures—you don't want to dig one out alone. When a tick attacks, it burrows its mouth into your skin. If any parts get left behind when you remove the tick, you could get an infection. So ask an adult to help with the plucking because you don't want to leave a tick head bobbing around in your body.

> **FAST FACT** • The American dog tick will wait on a blade of grass for two years for a feeding opportunity!

② Tweeze it.

To fight back after a tick attack, tweezers are your best weapon in the war against the tick inside you.

1. Have an adult sterilize a pair of tweezers by placing them in boiling water for five minutes.
2. After the tweezers cool down, look for the tick's head, then squeeze your tweezers around it as close to your skin as possible.
3. Quickly and firmly pull the tick's mouth (the part stuck in your skin) straight back until it's out of your skin. If any tick bits are left behind, dig them out with the tweezer, too.

BE AWARE • To avoid getting a tick, be sure to keep your skin covered when hiking in the deep woods. Tuck long pants into your socks, wear long sleeves, and put on a hat.

3 Clean and cover.

After the tick is out, clean the wound with soap and hot water—ticks can be *very* germy! Then put a bandage over the tick hole to keep it from getting infected.

4 Bag it.

After you've removed the tick, place it in a sealed plastic bag with a damp cotton ball to keep it moist. Bring the tick to your doctor. She may want to test it for a variety of tick-carrying diseases, like Lyme disease.

5 Do a tick check.

If you picked up one tick during your stroll through Ticktown, who knows how many other hitchhikers hopped on board. Check all the warm, hidden places on your body—like your armpits, the backs of your knees, in your butt crack, and behind your ears. And check Fido, too!

Other Vampiric Insects

Count Tickula and Louse the Impaler aren't the only bloodsucking bugs. Here are some other itty-bitty vamps itching to get their teeth into you.

- **Fleas.** These small, high-jumping insects drink the blood of animals and people, and can be *very* hard to get rid of because of their tininess and speed.

- **Mosquitoes.** They're not just annoying, these flying blood sponges can also be deadly! Mosquitoes spread more diseases—like malaria—around the world than any other bug.

- **Bedbugs.** These draculas live inside your mattress and feed on your blood at night. And they can survive for more than one-and-a-half years between meals.

- **Kissing bugs.** It's one kiss you *never* want to get! These bloodsuckers will sneak up on you while you sleep and often bite you near the lips to get a drink of blood.

Appendix

GROSSEST HUMAN HABITS IN HISTORY

Cannibalism. Brains with a side of tonsils, anyone? Some cultures used to eat other people in a practice known as cannibalism. Tribes honored their relatives by eating them after they died, and other cultures celebrated the bravery of their enemies after a battle by eating their foes' organs.

Drinking Pee. People have been drinking their pee for 5,000 years. Some people do it for religious reasons (in ancient India, pee was believed to be purifying). Some people do it for beauty (in 17th-century France, women took pee baths to keep their skin youthful). Some people do it for health reasons (the Aztecs used pee to disinfect wounds). Other times it's for survival (like when sailors are lost at sea!).

Disgusting Dinner Behavior.

Before napkins were invented, diners in the Middle Ages wiped their hands on the tablecloth. They also used the tablecloth to wipe their faces and blow their noses. If that's not gross enough, the table linens were only washed every couple of months…

Poop and Pee…Out the Window.

Before toilets were common household fixtures, people pooped and peed into chamber pots, which had to be emptied by hand. In most cities, this meant the chamber pots were dumped right out the window.

Tossing Trash Out the Window.

When poop and pee wasn't being tossed out windows, food scraps, old clothes, and all other trash was dumped onto the street. All of this garbage made for a breeding ground for diseases, including the Black Death (see page 67).

GROSS PRACTICAL JOKES

How to Make (and Use) Fake Snot

What you need:
- Large coffee mug
- 1/2 cup (120 milliliters) hot tap water
- 1 teaspoon (2 grams or 1/3 of packet) unflavored gelatin powder
- Dark molasses

To make the snot:

1. Fill the mug with the hot water. Add the gelatin and stir until dissolved.
2. Slowly add the molasses until the mixture is pale brown.
3. Add more water, continuing to stir until you get the room-temperature snot consistency just right.

To use: Place a big glob of the fake snot in the palm of your hand. Then find a family member or friend and pretend to sneeze into your hands. Groan, then open your hand to show the massive glob of "snot" you just blew out. Wipe a little of your home-brewed snot onto your face and hair. Guaranteed gross-out!

How to Make (and Use) Fake Puke

What you need:
- 1 can of chunky vegetable soup
- Large coffee mug
- Milk

To make the puke:

1. Empty half of the soup into the coffee mug.
2. Add milk to the mug slowly, stirring until the mixture begins to look like puke.
3. Taste your homemade gut chunks to make sure you can handle having the mixture in your mouth.

To use: Tell a friend or family member to meet you in your kitchen. Before they come in, take a big sip of your fake puke—but not too much. You want your cheeks to look like their normal size so nobody suspects you have anything in your mouth. Once the person walks in, start heaving like you're about to throw up and then hurl right into the sink.

How to Make (and Use) Fake Poop

What you need:
- Handful of dry dog food
- 2 plastic shopping bags
- 1 small can of wet dog food
- Large mixing bowl
- Large spoon
- Scissors

To make the poop:

1. Put the dry dog food into one of the plastic bags. Be sure to get all the air out of the bag before tying it off.
2. Place the bag on a counter or cutting board.
3. Use the bottom of the wet dog food can to lightly crush the dog food in the bag until it's the consistency of coarse sand.
4. Empty the can of dog food into the mixing bowl.
5. Add the crushed dog food to the wet dog food.
6. Mix the wet and dry food with the spoon until it's well combined. You now have a fake-poop mixture.
7. Spoon the fake poop into the second bag.
8. Push the fake poop into one corner of the bag, be sure to get all the air out, and then tie off the bag as close to the poop as possible. With scissors, cut a small hole about the size of a quarter.

To use: Take your poop dispenser and head outside. When you find a good location, like a nearby curb, gently squeeze the bag to squirt out a fake turd. Loop it around in a tight spiral to make a convincing pile of poo.

How to Make (and Use) Fake Blood

What you need:
- Large coffee mug
- 1 tablespoon (5 grams) cocoa powder
- 1/3 cup (120 milliliters) warm water
- 3 tablespoons (45 milliliters) corn syrup
- 10 to 20 drops red food coloring
- Paper towel

To make the blood:

1. Add the cocoa powder and water to the coffee mug. Mix well. Blend in the corn syrup and food coloring (add drops until you reach desired color).
2. Skim any bubbles or cocoa powder off the top with a paper towel, and your fake blood should be ready to spill.

To use: Place some fake blood on your face, like a wound, and splatter some on an old T-shirt to give your friend or family member a gory shock!

About the Experts

These experts reviewed select tips in this handbook and offered good advice on all things gross.

Lisa Polak is a scientist with degrees in animal biology and molecular genetics who has worked as an animal researcher and handler for more than fifteen years. For the last five years, she's worked at the Propsect Park Zoo in Brooklyn, New York, where she has been peed and pooped on by countless animals, from alligators to monkeys.

Renee Sherman has worked as a psychologist for the New York Department of Education for more than a decade. She helps kids in public schools deal with a wide range of issues, from first-day jitters to the many gross things they might see during an average school day.

Dr. Philippa Gordon is a neighborhood pediatrician in Brooklyn, New York. She grew up in England and South Africa and was educated in Maine and New York City.

Matthew Hall is a doctor who graduated from the University of Illinois College of Medicine. He will complete his residency in Radiation Oncology at City of Hope National Medical Center in Duarte, California.

About the Authors

David Borgenicht is the creator and coauthor of all of the books in the Worst-Case Scenario Survival Handbook series and the president and publisher of Quirk Books. In sixth grade, after drinking an excessive amount of hot chocolate and orange juice, he learned he was prone to carsickness. His soon-to-be ex-girlfriend learned that, too. The hard way.

The grossest thing that ever happened to **Nathaniel Marunas** was at his tenth birthday party when his best friend amazed everyone by drinking orange soda through his nose with a straw. When pizza was served, the glasses got mixed up, and Nathaniel drank most of the nostril soda before realizing his terrible mistake. He hasn't touched a drop of orange soda since.

As a child, **Robin Epstein** was so intrigued by seeing someone projectile vomit in a Chinese restaurant, it made her spontaneously vomit herself. She's had a tough time with hot-and-sour soup ever since.

About the Illustrator
Chuck Gonzales is very pleased to be involved with another Worst-Case Scenario Junior edition. His grossest experience as a kid was having to save his brother, who was using the restroom at the time, from a nasty scorpion.